THE MONSTERS WHO DIED
A MYSTERY ABOUT DINOSAURS

COWARD-McCANN, INC. NEW YORK

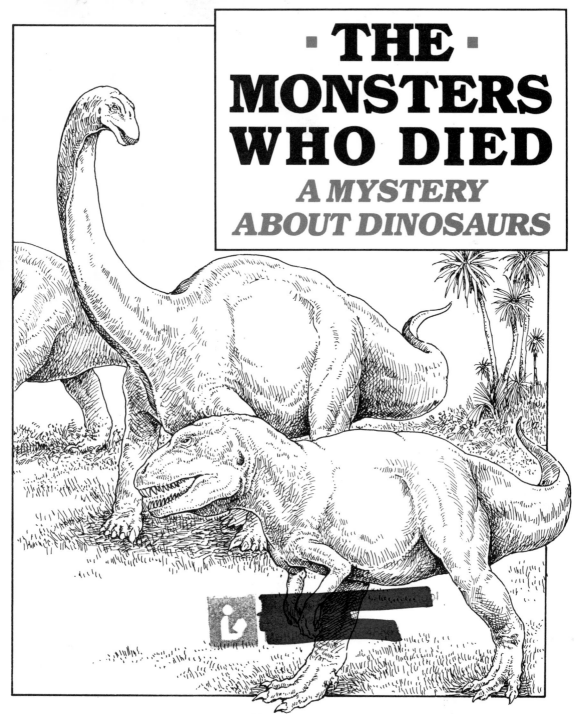

· THE ·
MONSTERS
WHO DIED
A MYSTERY
ABOUT DINOSAURS

BY VICKI COBB · ILLUSTRATED BY GREG WENZEL

For Dara,
Devoted dinosaur lover

Text copyright © 1983 by Vicki Cobb

Illustrations copyright © 1983 by Greg Wenzel

Printed in the United States of America

Library of Congress Cataloging in Publication Data

Cobb, Vicki. The monsters who died.
Includes index.
Summary: Discusses the methods used by paleontol-
ogists to decipher clues found in ancient bones and
fossils which provide our only means of learning
how dinosaurs lived and then became extinct.
1. Dinosaurs—Juvenile literature.
[1. Dinosaurs. 2. Paleontology. 3. Fossils]
I. Wenzel, Gregory C., ill. II. Title.
QE862.D5C62   1983   567.9'1   82-14252
ISBN 0-698-20571-5
Sixth Impression

CONTENTS

THE MONSTERS WHO DIED
A MYSTERY ABOUT DINOSAURS

1

The Puzzle:

Bones in Stone

About two hundred years ago, a skull was discovered buried in stone. It was not your ordinary skull, not by a long shot! The jaw was 4 feet long and it was full of daggerlike teeth. It was very clear that the skull had once been part of a huge and dangerous creature. It was also clear that there was nothing alive quite like it.

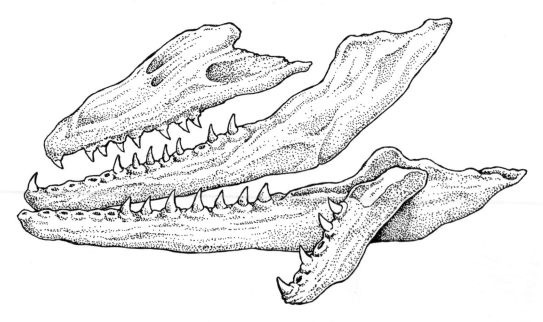

As you might imagine, the strange skull caused great excitement. It was the first piece of hard evidence from the past that proved very large animals had existed. Monsters once had been real!

Scientists studied the skull and scratched their heads. What kind of monster was it? There was one obvious clue: the shape of the skull. It looked like an enormous enlargement of the skulls of certain living lizards. So the scientists figured that the monster had to be some kind of giant lizard.

9

That was one of many questions asked about the skull. Here are some others:

How big was this giant lizard? A 4-foot jaw could belong only to a lizard at least 25 feet long. That's about as long as a good-sized living room. The largest modern lizard is only 8 feet long.

What kind of food did this creature eat? The teeth were designed for one thing, and one thing only: killing. There were no flat teeth for chewing, only sharp teeth for biting. So the monster must have killed other animals and swallowed them in one gulp. Fearsome, indeed!

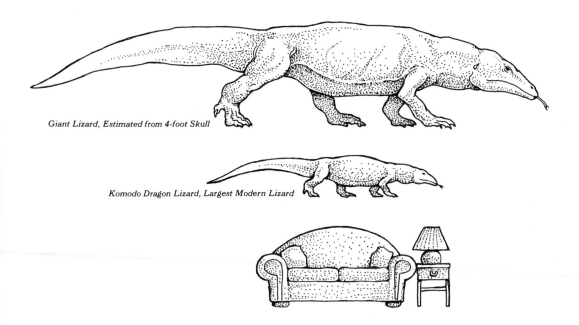

Giant Lizard, Estimated from 4-foot Skull

Komodo Dragon Lizard, Largest Modern Lizard

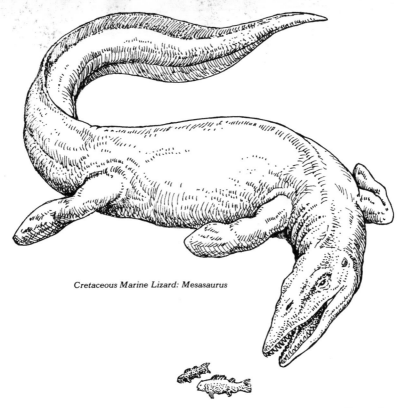

Cretaceous Marine Lizard: Mesasaurus

Where did this monster live? The stone surrounding the skull gave the answer to this question. It was chalk, and we know that chalk forms only at the bottom of the sea. Layers of seashells settled there. The weight built up and pressed down on the lower layers. These became a soft rock known as chalk or *limestone*. Limestone around the skull could only mean that the monster had lived in the sea. Limestone is used to make buildings. The skull was discovered by limestone cutters.

When did this sea monster live? Again the rock gave the answer. The limestone was in a mountain. But remember that limestone forms at the bottom of the sea. How did it get in a mountain? The answer is: through several steps. First there must have been a sea. Shells fell to the bottom to become limestone. The sea flowed somewhere else as the earth forced the ocean floor upwards, forming a mountain. Such changes take hundreds of millions of years. The monster must have lived millions and millions of years ago, when it was swimming in a sea that disappeared.

As it turned out, the skull in stone was the first of many discoveries of ancient bones of monsters. Once there were lots of different kinds of the giant beasts around. This was so long ago that there were no people yet on earth. The giant beasts were the largest, strongest creatures. There were so many of them that they ruled the earth.

Why did the sea monster die? Perhaps this monster was wounded when it was swimming. It could not reach the surface of the water for air and it drowned. Since the rest of the skeleton was missing, there were no other clues to this monster's death. But the events that led to this monster's death are not an important question. The big mystery is this: Why are they *all* dead? Why aren't there any such powerful creatures on the face of the earth today? What killed *all* the great monsters of the past?

These questions have kept scientists busy for two hundred years. Scientists are the detectives investigating the mystery. The case is far from closed.

This book tells part of the story.

2

The Clues:

Digging Up the Evidence

As in all mysteries, some clues are better than others. Bones are the main clues to the mystery of the monsters who died and they come in all shapes and sizes. There are broken bones that have to be fitted together. There are whole bones that have to be fitted into a skeleton. And once in a while there is a complete skeleton. That's the best clue we can hope for.

Skeletons are, after all, only part of what once were living, breathing animals. Scientists' imaginations have to put muscles and skin on those old bones. Sometimes there is a piece of preserved skin around to give a clue to the outside appearance. But most of the time the pictures you look at of these ancient beasts are just a good guess.

There are other clues. Monster footprints have been found preserved in rock. Just think, millions of years ago a

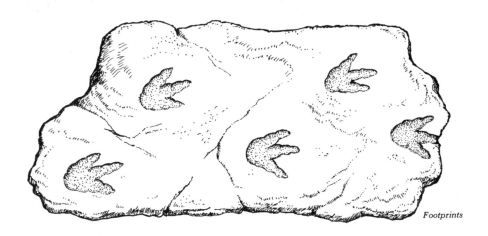

Footprints

beast walked through some mud that later hardened into rock. The record of that moment has survived a mind-boggling passage of time.

Eggs turned to stone are yet another clue: unhatched baby monsters millions of years old!

The scientists who work to solve puzzles from these clues are called *paleontologists*. They begin by getting their hands dirty digging in the earth for pieces from the past.

Fossilized Eggs

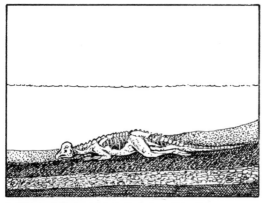

1. The dead dinosaur sinks to the bottom of the river.

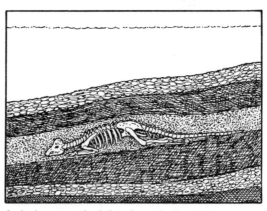

2. As time passes, the skeleton is completely covered with sediment.

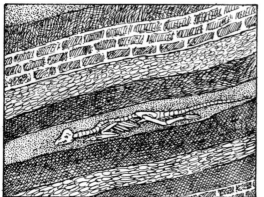

3. More sediment accumulates, and the skeleton is mineralized.

4. The fossilized skeleton is exposed today by erosion.

They dig for the rocks that once were sand, mud, shells, or leaves. Long ago the bodies of animals were trapped in these materials. Over a period of time the soft parts of the bodies rotted away. Rock hardened around the bones. Sometimes the bone itself turned into rock. In these rocks we can easily

16

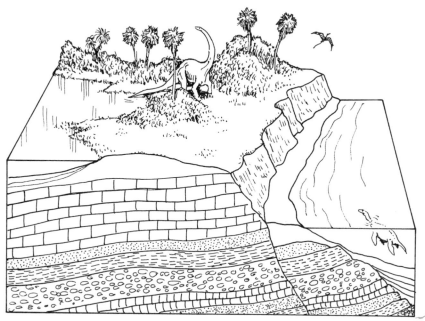

Cutaway Diagram of the Earth, Showing the Different Layers

see the shapes of the bones as they once were. All these bones from the past are called *fossils*.

The search for fossils is like a treasure hunt. Paleontologists set up camps near rocks that are likely to contain fossils. Then, with picks and shovels, they dig into earth's history.

The rock itself is a clue to the age of a fossil. Rock forms in layers. It is easy to see the layers. They are like stripes. The deep layers formed first so they are the oldest rocks with the top layers the youngest. There is often a clear division between layers. Each one can mark off a time period.

Sometimes the earth's crust moves and shifts. The rock layers are folded into waves. Weather wears away the upper layers. Sometimes a paleontologist gets lucky and finds a fossil that has been brought to the surface.

Imagine the excitement when a large fossil, like a dinosaur skeleton, is discovered. Before anything is moved, scientists take a picture of it where they found it, just like detectives at the scene of a murder.

Then they cut the skeleton out of the rocks and send it to a laboratory or a museum for study. Digging up the evidence is work! Some fossils weigh tons. Each piece is carefully labeled and protected with packing before it is shipped.

The dirty work doesn't stop in the lab. The fossil bones have to be separated from the rock that surrounds them. Sometimes the work is so delicate that dentist's tools are used.

Finally the skeleton is ready to be put together. Each bone is put in its correct place. Usually there are bones missing. So paleontologists make models of bones shaped like bones of similar animals alive today. They also may use fossil bones from other skeletons.

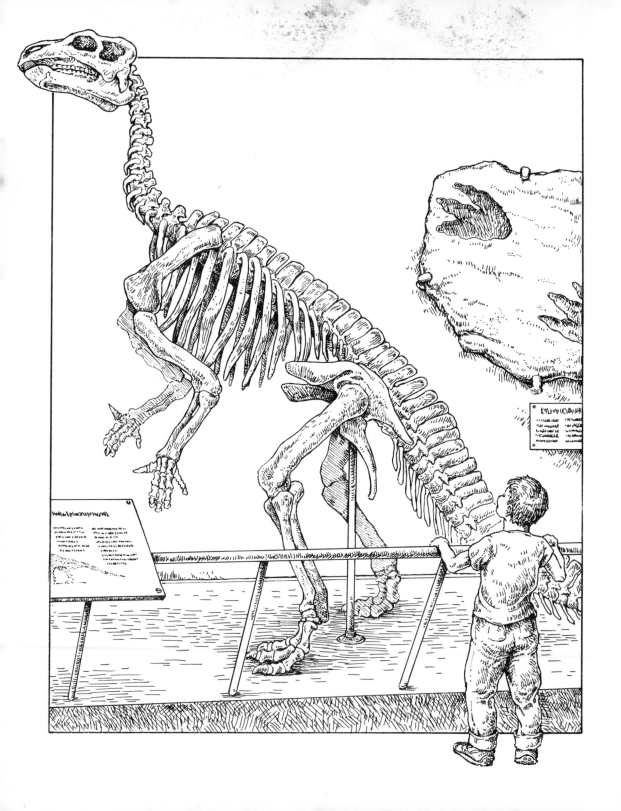

At last there is a complete skeleton. One part of the puzzle is solved. But do you think that stops the guesses and arguments? No way! Now scientists try and figure out what the living, breathing beast was like. They look for the places on the bones where muscles attached. They look at similar living animals to figure out the shape of the muscles. The shape of all the muscles gives the shape of the animal. Then scientists make guesses about the skin covering. Today's lizards have scaly skin. Some fossil skin is also scaly. So scientists figure that ancient monsters were covered with the same kind of skin. So much for how they looked.

Scientists also want to know how they lived, what they ate, where they roamed and how they reproduced. If we know how they lived, maybe we'll know why they died. Part of an answer always means new questions. So the search goes on.

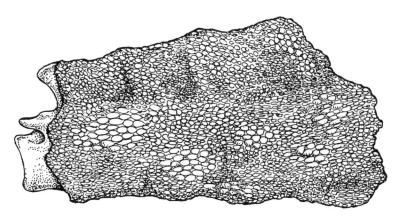

Fossilized Skin

3

The Detective Work:

Putting the Pieces Together

About fifty years after the clue of the skull in stone, there was another big discovery. Pieces of a dead monster were found by the side of a road in England. Not much was found. Only some flat teeth, a spike that looked like a horn, and some toe bones.

Now teeth and toe bones don't seem very exciting. But wait. They only happened to be the largest teeth and toe bones anyone had ever seen. The teeth and bones were the first pieces of evidence of the biggest kind of monster ever to roam the land . . . the dinosaur! The skull from the sea monster was a distant cousin of dinosaurs.

What a challenge to figure out what the first dinosaur looked like from these few clues! The spike made scientists think that the beast was like a rhinoceros with a horn on its nose. The toe bones reminded someone of a hippopotamus.

But the teeth turned out to be the truly important clue. One paleontologist noticed that they were shaped exactly like the teeth of an iguana (i-GWAN-a), a modern-day lizard from Central America.

The main difference between the fossil teeth and those of the living iguana was, of course, size. The fossil teeth were 20 times larger than the iguana teeth. Today's iguana is a lizard about 5 feet long. Was the dead monster 20 times larger? Was it almost 100 feet long?

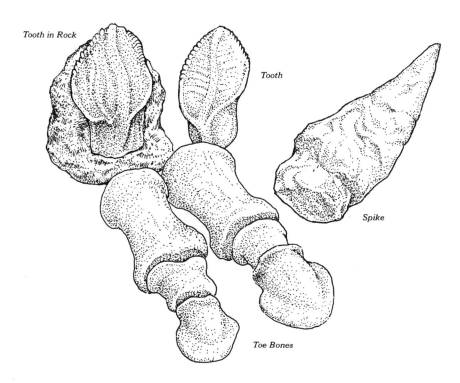

Tooth in Rock

Tooth

Spike

Toe Bones

Scientists had to find another clue to get the answer. Luckily, they found a few back bones near the place where they found the teeth. These could only belong to a beast 25 feet long. Not the size of a house pet!

They named the dinosaur *Iguanodon* (i-GWAN-o-don), which means "iguana tooth." An artist worked with paleontologists to build a life-sized model for a museum in England.

Modern Iguana Lizard

Early Reconstruction of an Iguanodon

The model builders thought the Iguanodon walked on four feet and that the spiked bone belonged at the end of its nose. This is how they thought the Iguanodon looked in 1853. Later scientists discovered there was a lot wrong with this picture.

Turn the page to see how we think the Iguanodon looks today.

25

Behold THE IGUANODON!

This is how we now believe the Iguanodon looked. This idea is based on more than thirty complete Iguanodon skeletons. The spiked bone has been moved from the nose to the thumb. It was probably used as a weapon for defense since the shape of the teeth tell us it was a plant-eater.

The Iguanodon walked on two legs and stood about two stories high. It was a medium-sized dinosaur, as dinosaurs go. The Iguanodon's heavy tail was probably held straight out in the air for balance when it walked and was used as a third leg when it rested.

Perhaps new evidence will turn up to change this picture.

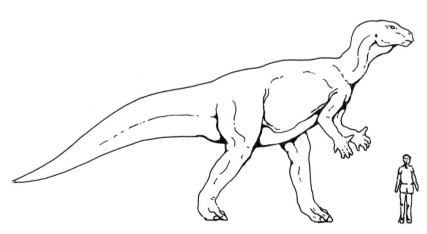

All the pictures of the dinosaurs show the beast's size in comparison with that of a 4-foot-tall child.

4
Other Victims

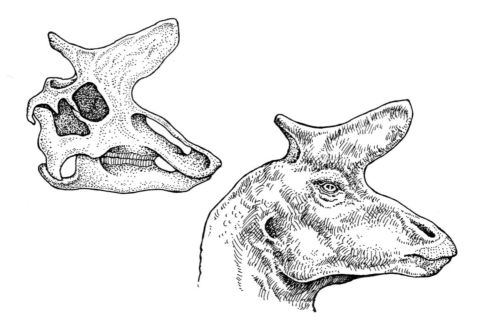

Scientists have drawn pictures of many dinosaurs based on the discoveries of lots of skeletons. These dinosaurs are dead, all victims of some killer in nature. Get familiar with the evidence and the pictures. We'll lay it out for you.

Evidence of the "Thunder Reptile"

These remains are much bigger than those of the Iguanodon. Scientists puzzled over complete skeletons with:
  a thigh bone as tall as a man and as thick as a tree trunk
  3 curved claws on the hind feet
  one curved claw on the front foot
  a small skull with very weak teeth and a larger skull with
      pencil-like teeth.
  fossil footprints one yard apart
  fossil tracks of just the front feet

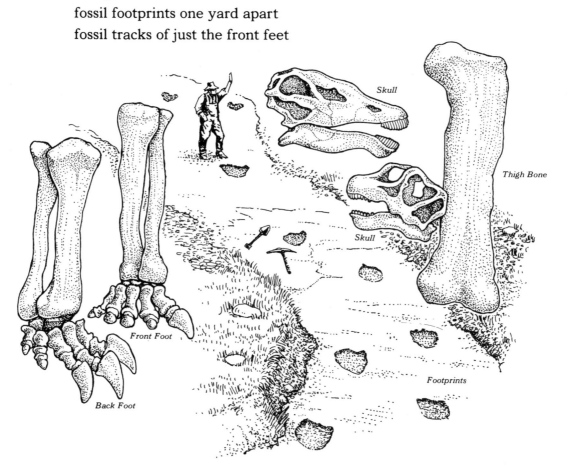

Skull

Thigh Bone

Skull

Front Foot

Footprints

Back Foot

Behold the BRONTOSAURUS!

Everything about this beast was supersized! Paleontologists figure it weighed about 20 tons or as much as 6 elephants. It was named *Brontosaurus* (bronto-SAWR-us), meaning "thunder reptile," because it must have made thunderous noise as it tramped over the ground. Did it live in water or on land? The fossil footprints of the front feet only are evidence that the monster lived in water. Its hind feet probably floated along behind. Perhaps Brontosaurus lived in shallow lakes. The water would have helped support the tremendous weight.

Later studies have shown us that the leg bones were probably strong enough to support the beast on land, too, but we're still not sure.

And now, here's the story of the head. For more than fifty years the head of the Brontosaurus was thought to be very small compared to the rest of its body. The entire skull was smaller than one of its neck bones. There was room only for a tiny brain. If this skull truly belonged to this dinosaur, the beast must have been very slow and stupid. Its size must have protected it from its enemies. Clearly it could not outrun or outsmart them. Some scientists thought that the small skull didn't belong on the body. It was found some distance away from the rest of the skeleton. Since it was the only skull they found at that time, it was put on the end of the neck.

What about the very weak teeth in the skull? They seem

to be good for chewing only soft food, such as water plants. The long neck of the dinosaur would have allowed it to nibble treetops like a giraffe. Leaves are also soft food. Evidence for both kinds of feeding, on land and in water, exists. But you get in trouble when you start thinking how much a beast of this size would have to eat.

Scientists' First Idea of How the Brontosaurus Looked

An elephant eats between 400 and 800 pounds of food a day and spends about 18 hours doing it. Suppose Brontosaurus, six times the size of an elephant, had a similar appetite. It would have to spend more than 24 hours a day eating. Impossible! Besides, its tiny mouth doesn't seem to be built for so much work.

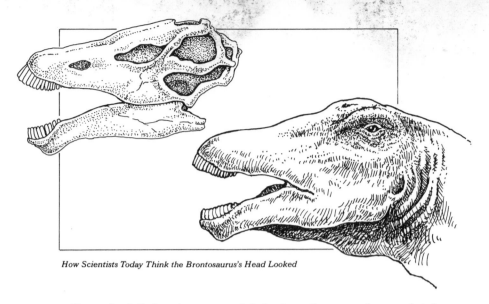

How Scientists Today Think the Brontosaurus's Head Looked

Surprise! Scientists now think that they made a mistake about the head. The new head is now thought to be much larger than the one that sat on top of the skeleton for so long. The first Brontosaurus skeleton, found in Wyoming, didn't have a head. The scientist who discovered it needed a head, so he used one he found about four miles away. A few years later, two other Brontosaurus skeletons were found in Utah. A large skull was found on top of the neck of one skeleton and another smaller skull was found nearby. When the skulls were shipped back to the lab, they were mixed up. The smaller skull was thought to belong to the beast. It was like the one they already had. The mistake was discovered only recently when old letters by the paleontologists describing the skeletons were studied by today's scientists.

It seems that one big mystery about the Brontosaurus has just been cleared up.

34

Evidence of the "Big-Arm" Lizard

Believe it or not, there was evidence of a dinosaur bigger than Brontosaurus!

Scientists puzzled over these remains:
arm bones (forelegs) over 6 feet long
neck bones each over 2 feet long
arm bones longer than the hind leg bones
nostrils on top of the snout

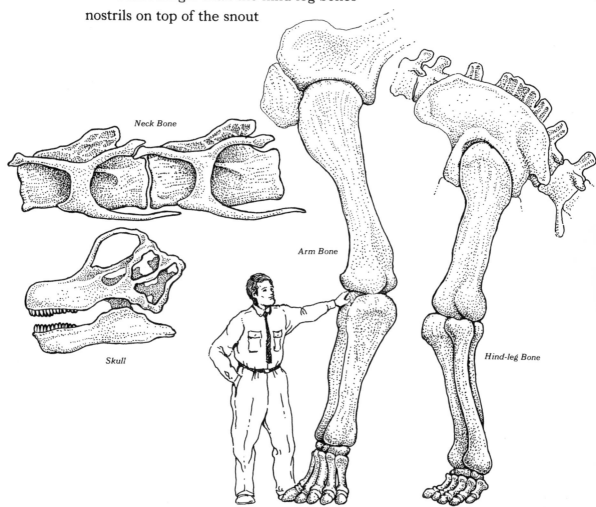

Neck Bone

Arm Bone

Skull

Hind-leg Bone

Behold THE BRACHIOSAURUS!

No question, this is a giant among giants! *Brachiosaurus* (brake-e-o-SAWR-us), meaning "big-arm lizard," got its name because its front legs were longer than its hind legs—a switch if there ever was one. Most dinosaurs walked on the hind legs only and used their tiny forelegs for grasping.

Until recently Brachiosaurus held the record as the largest dinosaur. It weighed 80 tons or as much as four Brontosaurs. But now there is a shoulder blade larger than a man. Scientists say it belongs to an even larger beast called the *Supersaurus*. It may have weighed 100 tons and was built like a Brachiosaurus.

Here's what they think they both looked like. The shoulder of a Brachiosaurus was nearly two stories high. Its head was two stories above the shoulder on a snakelike neck. It walked on all fours in order to support its heavy body. Its teeth tell us it was a plant-eater.

Supersaurus

Brachiosaurus

What about the nostrils on top of the snout? At first scientists thought that the animal walked along the bottoms of lakes breathing air with their snouts at the surface, like crocodiles. But further thinking rejected this idea. Here's why. If the Brachiosaurus were completely underwater, the water would weigh heavily on its chest. The crush of the water would be so great that it would have to have very powerful breathing muscles. The skeleton of a Brachiosaurus doesn't seem to be built to have such muscles. Experts now believe that the Brachiosaurus, like its cousin Brontosaurus, walked on land and waded in shallow lakes.

Evidence of the Armored Dinosaur

This monster had some really strange parts. The skeletons included:

20 bony plates lying along the spine

2 pairs of spikes near the tail

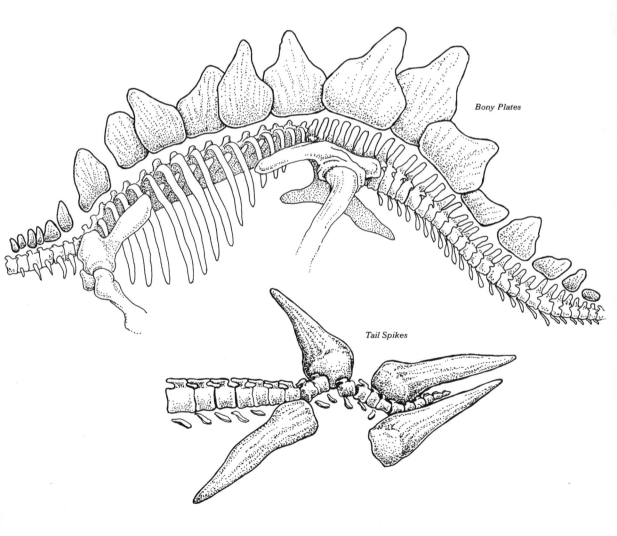

Bony Plates

Tail Spikes

Behold THE STEGOSAURUS!

Built like a living tank, this dinosaur came with plates. So scientists named it *Stegosaurus* (steg-o-SAWR-us), meaning "plate lizard."

Scientists figured that the two pairs of spikes belonged on the tail. The Stegosaurus could defend itself by swinging its tail as a weapon. It was a plant-eater and needed protection from the meat-eaters.

The Stegosaur's mystery was its plates. They were very large, almost 36 inches across. How had they been arranged on the body of the animal? After much arguing, experts finally agreed that Stegosaurus had plates standing up along its spine in two rows. They were not lined up in pairs but overlapped each other.

For many years, scientists believed that the plates were for protection. Recently, they've taken a closer look at the fossils and come up with another idea. The plates are full of tiny holes that could have contained blood vessels. Blood could have circulated through the plates.

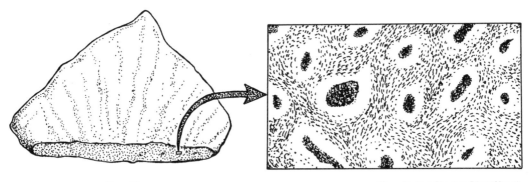

Bony Plate   *Cross Section Showing Blood Vessels*

If so, the plates may have had another use. They could have cooled off the body of the Stegosaurus, acting like a radiator sending heat into the air. No modern reptile does this. They all have to go somewhere cool to cool off.

This idea is exciting to scientists. At the present time they divide animals neatly into two groups. The "cold-blooded" group includes all fish, amphibians (frogs and toads), and reptiles. The body temperature, warm or cool, depends on the temperature of the animal's surroundings. The "warm-

blooded" group, which includes birds and mammals, keeps body temperature pretty much the same, no matter how surrounding temperatures change. If the Stegosaurus could regulate its body heat with its plates, it could have been warm-blooded. Or it could be a "missing link" between the cold-blooded and warm-blooded animals.

This could prove to be an important idea in solving the mystery. You'll see why as you read on.

42

Evidence of the Three-Horned Dinosaur

The skeleton of this strange-looking beast came complete with:

a skull with 3 horns
side horns measuring up to 3 feet in length
a bony collar around the neck
a 25-foot skeleton

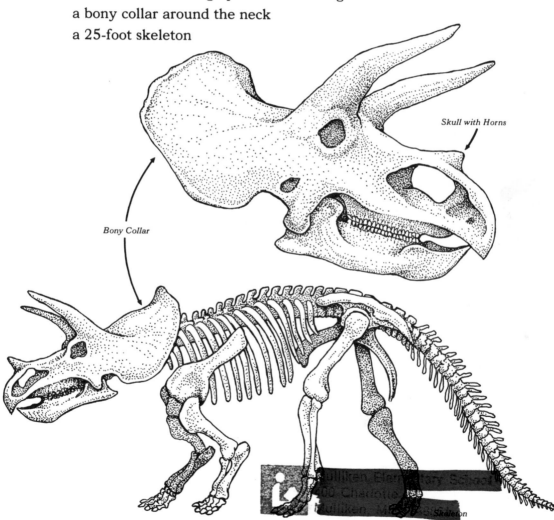

Skull with Horns

Bony Collar

Behold THE TRICERATOPS!

The three big horns on the face gave this dinosaur its name. *Triceratops* (try-SER-a-tops) could have been the rhinoceros of dinosaurs.

Compared to other dinosaurs, the Triceratops was not very large, only somewhat bigger than a modern elephant. But the horned head with its bony collar was huge, 8 feet long. It took up almost one-third of the length of the body.

The Triceratops did not use its horns to kill for food. It had a toothless, hooked beak that was probably used for ripping up plants. There were teeth at the back of its jaw that worked like scissors. The bony collar was probably the place where its powerful jaw muscles were attached. The whole setup of the mouth made scientists think that the Triceratops ate very tough plants, like reeds.

Meat-eating dinosaurs must have found the Triceratops fearsome. All it had to do to defend itself was to lower its head and face its enemy. Any animal that attacked Triceratops ran the risk of getting gored by its horns.

But the Triceratops' horns were no defense against whatever killed the dinosaurs. It was among the last of the dinosaurs and its extinction is dramatically told in stone. At one time there were herds of Triceratops roaming the earth. Lots of fossils prove this. But as the layers of fossil rock get closer to the present, there are fewer and fewer monsters. Suddenly there is a layer, only a few inches thick, that has no dinosaur fossils at all. Inches in fossil rock stand for a very

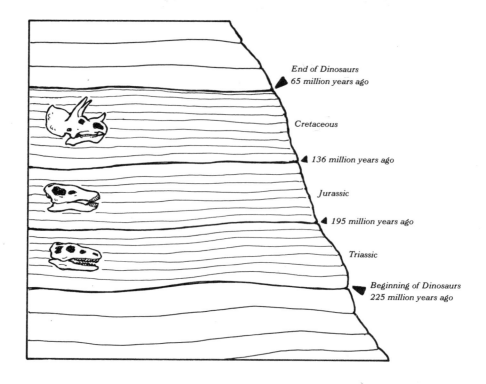

End of Dinosaurs
65 million years ago

Cretaceous

136 million years ago

Jurassic

195 million years ago

Triassic

Beginning of Dinosaurs
225 million years ago

short time in earth's history. Dinosaurs did not gradually die out. They were victims of some mysterious cause of death in as little as 100,000 years, a brief moment in earth's history.

Triceratops was the last of the plant-eating dinosaurs. The next dinosaur you'll meet was a meat-eater and the Triceratops' worst enemy. It also disappeared from the earth. Perhaps the last of the dinosaurs can explain why they all died. Scientists give them a lot of attention.

Evidence of the King of Killers

These bones were the stuff of nightmares. There was no question that they belonged to the king of killers. The skeleton had:

a 4-foot skull with 60 double-edged, swordlike teeth

a skeleton 20 feet tall

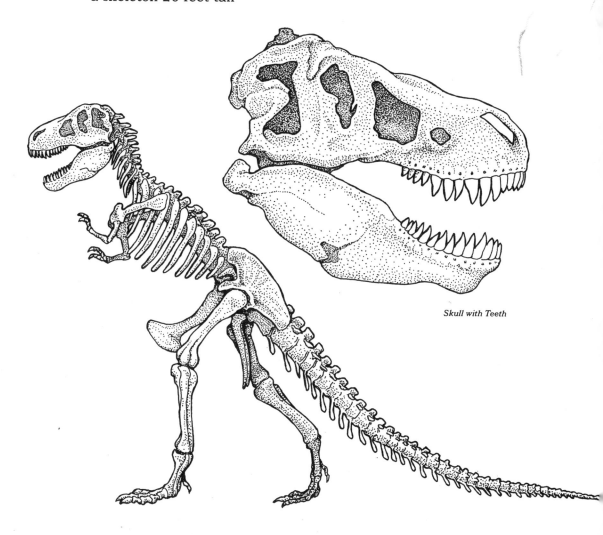

Skull with Teeth

Behold TYRANNOSAURUS REX!

This monster is usually voted the one most likely to be feared. Its name means "king of the tyrant lizards." *Tyrannosaurus* (tie-ran-o-SAWR-us) *rex* was almost 50 feet long and stood two stories high. Its head was clearly built for killing. The teeth were designed to tear flesh to be swallowed without chewing.

The forelegs were tiny and seem to have no purpose. They were so short that the beast couldn't scratch its nose if it itched. A possible explanation is that the forelegs were used to help Tyrannosaurus to its feet after it had been resting on its belly. The claws of the forelegs dug into the ground to keep the head from sliding forward. Meanwhile, the rear end was struggling to stand up. Not a very kinglike position for the king of dinosaurs!

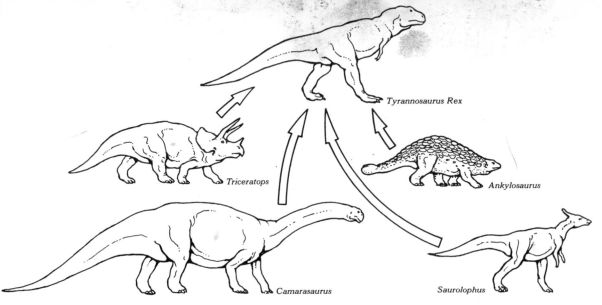

Tyrannosaurus Rex

Triceratops

Ankylosaurus

Camarasaurus

Saurolophus

Tyrannosaurus ate plant-eating animals, including Triceratops. But how much did it eat? One way of guessing is to look at the number of animals in the groups it feeds on. There are, for example, many more plant-eating antelopes than there are lions that eat them. The sizes of these two groups are a very rough measure of the lions' appetite. The size of the antelope group must be large enough to feed the lions and still survive. Cold-blooded animals need less food than warm-blooded ones. There are many more fossils of plant-eating dinosaurs than there are of Tyrannosaurus. This suggests that Tyrannosaurus may have had a huge appetite, like warm-blooded animals. Perhaps it *was* a warm-blooded animal. Interesting. . . .

You would expect Tyrannosaurus to disappear at about the same time as Triceratops. Without the plant-eaters to feed on, Tyrannosaurus rex couldn't survive either.

Evidence of the Age of Dinosaurs

There are dinosaur fossils in rocks 200 million years old. The last fossils are found in rocks 65 million years old. Dinosaur fossils have been found on every continent, and in the Arctic Circle. We have recovered hundreds of dinosaur skeletons. Some are as small as cats; others are as tall as buildings.

In spite of their differences, all dinosaurs are alike in certain ways. They are reptiles. Their skulls all have five holes where muscles attached. The skulls are small compared to the rest of the body.

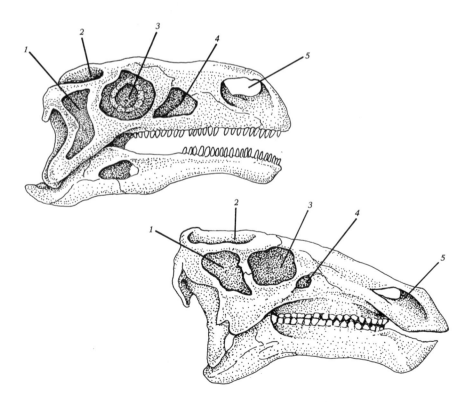

Behold THE DINOSAUR WORLD!

ALLOSAURUS (al-lo-SAWR-us), the "hunter reptile," whose main food was the giant plant-eaters. Brontosaurus was his meat!

ANKYLOSAURUS (an-kyle-o-SAWR-us) was the "curved lizard," so named for its curved ribs. It was the "turtle" of the dinosaur world.

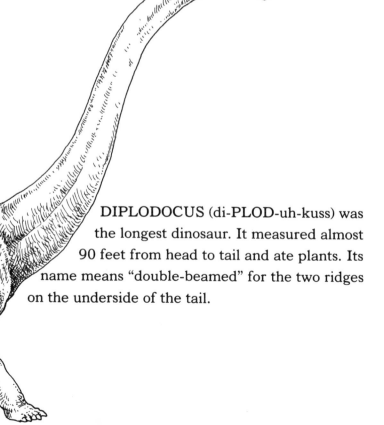

DIPLODOCUS (di-PLOD-uh-kuss) was the longest dinosaur. It measured almost 90 feet from head to tail and ate plants. Its name means "double-beamed" for the two ridges on the underside of the tail.

DEINONYCHUS (dine-o-NYE-chus), meaning "terrible claw." Small, swift, and deadly, this creature killed with a kick of one of its hind feet.

CORYTHOSAURUS (kor-ith-o-SAWR-us), the "helmet lizard," was a duck-billed monster. It had as many as 200 grinding teeth in the back of its strange mouth, perfect for turning reeds into mush.

At the same time there were a few cousins of dinosaurs around, making this period the Age of Reptiles.

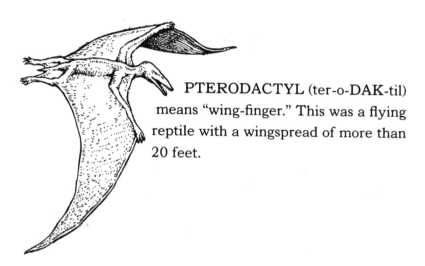

PTERODACTYL (ter-o-DAK-til) means "wing-finger." This was a flying reptile with a wingspread of more than 20 feet.

ICTHYOSAURUS (ik-thee-o-SAWR-us) was a fishlike reptile.

5

Filling in the Picture:

Possible Solutions

There are a few clues that directly point to the death of the dinosaurs. First is the disappearance of dinosaur fossils in rocks that formed less than 65 million years ago. The fossils date the time of extinction quite exactly. Dinosaur eggs also show the decline of dinosaurs. Eggs 70 million years old and older have thick shells. The shells from the last five million years got thinner and thinner. Dinosaurs were not as healthy. It showed in their eggshells. Thin eggshells are not such good protection. Many young dinosaurs never hatched. The poor health of the parents affected the young.

Fossil records show that many other living things died about the same time as dinosaurs and their cousins. Many sea animals died. Tropical plants on land were replaced by pine trees.

What caused such widespread death? One scientist offered this theory: Dinosaurs were poisoned by eating flowering plants. However, the evidence showed that flowering plants appeared 50 million years before dinosaurs died. So this idea was knocked down. If flowering plants could kill, they would have killed sooner.

Some scientists think that a nearby star exploded and showered the earth with deadly radiation, killing all the dinosaurs. The trouble with this idea is that many animals did survive, like some early mammals, that should have died along with the dinosaurs.

The most popular theory is that the dinosaurs died when the climate became cooler. Dinosaurs were suited to living in tropical weather. They had no fur or feathers to protect them from cold. They were too big to burrow. As winters grew colder, different groups of dinosaurs died off until there were none. Did any of their relatives survive?

Some scientists think so. Perhaps the descendants of dinosaurs are today's birds. It's hard to imagine a Brontosaurus as a relative of a pigeon. But there is a missing link. It is a fossil creature called *Archeopteryx* (ark-ee-OP-ter-icks).

For twenty years after the first Archeopteryx skeleton was discovered, scientists thought it was a small dinosaur. After all, its skull had those five holes typical of all dinosaur skulls. Then they thought it was a bird because it had two features common to birds, namely, a wishbone and feathers.

The plates of the Stegosaurus, the appetite of Tyranno-

saurus, and the feathers on Archeopteryx all add weight to the idea of warm-blooded dinosaurs. Feathers are necessary to keep in body heat. An animal with feathers could survive a change to a colder climate. Archeopteryx could be the ancestor of all birds.

What could have caused such a quick change in climate? Perhaps it was an ice age. Perhaps it was an explosion of a nearby star that showered the earth's atmosphere with climate-changing radiation.

Recently a new idea made news. Two scientists in California blame the death of the dinosaurs on an asteroid that crashed into the earth. They suggest that an asteroid, which is a chunk of rock, about three miles in diameter hit the earth. The collision, according to their calculations, created a crater about sixty miles across and really raised the dust. In fact, they believe that so much dust was sent into the air that the sunlight was blocked for at least three years. During this time the dying started. Green plants died, plant-eaters died, meat-eaters died. Only animals that could eat nuts, seeds, or rotten plants survived.

These scientists say that after a while the dust settled, and they claim they've found it. That is the main evidence for their theory. But no one has yet found the crater that would add to their evidence. People are keeping their eyes open, however.

Mystery will always surround the dinosaurs. We may

never know what color they were, or how long a life-span they had, or how fast they grew from egg to adult. But there is still evidence out there waiting to be discovered. New theories are sure to be suggested. There is still lots of detective work to be done. And it will be there when you grow up. Perhaps you will become one of the scientists investigating the mystery of the monsters who died. The more we understand about life and death in the past, the more we'll understand about life and death in the future. If you should join the search for answers, you will be welcome.

Index